Bones

Also by Angela Carole Brown

Trading Fours, 2005
The Assassination of Gabriel Champion, 2013
The Kidney Journals: Memoirs of a Desperate Lifesaver, 2014
Aleatory on the Radio, 2019
Viscera, 2019

Bones

Angela Carole Brown

HAIKU HOUSE

Bones

Published by Haiku House
First Edition
ISBN-13: 978-1-7337453-0-7

"Female Nude from the Rear View" 1958
Abstract Acrylic on Canvas by

Ted Brown

Ted Brown spent his life as an artist, his career specifically
as a graphic artist in the aerospace industry from
1962 until his retirement in 2002, and his time and love
as a man devoted to his family. Ted Brown died on
August 10, 2017, the year this collection was written.

Contents

Female Nude From the Rear View   13
Lost and Found   14
Are You Dreaming   16
We   18
The Steps Are Loose   20
In the Time Before Thought   22
They Always Remind Me of Butterflies   23
Equilibrium   25
Inflammation   28
Woodwork   29
Is There Room For Me Here?   31
Dancing   32
Children   34
Salt & Silt   36
His Hands   37
My Superior Beast   38
Duck & Weave   40
A Morning Cup   41
Wait   43
In This Room   47
Harbored   51
Splinters   53
Tribulation   54
Things Known   56
Our Kodachrome Life   59
Silence   60
Reaching Ears   62
SATC Moment   64
Penumbra   66
Elegy for the One More   74
Notes   76
Pull   78
Sing   79
Joon   80
Him   81
Uninvited   82
Concerto for Breath and Orchestra   84
A Talk with Death   88
But There   89
Nature After All   91
Knotty Little Demon   97
Holy Order   99
Motion Sickness   100
The Starting Bell   102
Tomorrow   104
Bones   106

Bones are not uniformly solid.
They include a tough matrix.

Female Nude From the Rear View

do you see her?
hiding among the blue trees
& shards of mustard delphiniums?
her forest of daggers. her splintered bones.
calling. demurring.
running. naked. away.
always away.
never toward.
she breaks & is broken.
she dances & is rounded.
her flesh, the ancestors.
her eyes, seldom seen.
weapons. pawns?
she calls out…

is there anybody out there?

tacky as milkweed stuck & yowling
she is the center of the universe & the outer rim,
which threatens to fold back into its own half-light.
that deadly curve at the buttocks.
right where lovers have placed their hands, uneasy.
she will fold you into her.
so, want to go. because you won't return.
hear her, if you can't see her, when she says…

like lennie
petting his poor doomed puppy to its death
because he loved it too much
i could kill you.

believe her.

Lost and Found
(written on January 1, 2018)

In 2017, I...
Lost my father.
Lost a brother, too, in a manner of speaking.
Found my voice as a poet.
Found my brother.
Endured whiplash, of both the literal and the emotional brand.
Thought about my father.
Blocked out the White Noise of the White House.
Stood in awe as my city burned, and a few others nearly drowned, while
feeling the haunting wail of a planet in trouble.
Witnessed the unfettered power of #metoo, and the spiritual
vacuum cleaner that got unleashed.
Watched "post-racial America" reveal its truest colors.
Fostered anxiety.
Lost my brother again.
Bonded with family in an unprecedented and crucial way.
Found baby bro yet again.
Learned to love and let go in equal measure.
Re-learned it every — single — damned — hardheaded — day.
Thought about my father.
Wrote about my father.
Held my dying kitty girl in my arms. Impossible.
Lost more and more beloveds in too heartbreaking a number.
Had a talk with Death. It was a Come-to-Jesus moment, with a few side-
eyes between us.
Wrote my 1st short story.
Wrote my 118th short story.
Felt my age.
Killed a plant.
Went vegan.
....ish.

Lived up to my hype.

Didn't live up to my hype.

Failed my hype miserably.

Decided that *hype* was not a word worthy of my time.

Ripped the meat from the bone with dripping teeth. Even the toughest will fall right off, if cooked just right.

Talked earnestly to my father, my mother, my stepfather, the ancestors, all who have left this earth but are never far, and who give me living tips daily.

Wrote these thoughts on the first day of the New Year, to usher out an old, usher in a new. To ritualize the idea of rebirth, renewal, and restoration, because I am a New Year baby; it is in my DNA to ritualize, to chant, to pray, to dance, to give auspiciousness to new beginnings and rites of passage, to participate in burning bowl rituals and labyrinth walks, to summon the rains and the gods, to howl at the moon, to burn sage, to close my eyes, shut off the valve and listen. Listen to the wind in the trees tell me what I need to know next, what I need to do next, how I need to sing next. And then I sing.

The very last thing I did in the very last moments of 2017 was sing.

As it has been since forever ago and auld lang syne.

I sang and sang.

And baby brother is home.

Nestled in all the love his family has to give.

We get to remember my father together.

All of us. Together.

So, here we are, New Year. Dancing around each other,
two cats circling, spines arched scoliotic like raised welts.
Be nice now.

Are You Dreaming

beautiful dreams?
Do your mumbles
& titters solve
puzzles
& crimes?

Have the skies
opened up &
taken you in?
Wrapped you
like a shawl?
Bundled you in
fevers of starlight
& comets?

Can you know
what lies ahead?
&
what road you'll
take to get there?

Is there magic in
your travels?
Light unburied
by black waters?

If so then plunge
your stakes
into the ground.

Heave your
blessings
outward.
Cleave a path
through the ice
but not
through love.

Shed the skin that
is sloughing off
in inches
& blunders
anyway
to make way
for poetry.

Live in the
never-ending
wonder
&
wander
there
never-ending.

This is where we
can meet again
touch foreheads
&
be one.

We

The first day of mourning came in early November.
Cloud cover. A foreboding of the year to come.
For some, a day of triumph. A new era ushered in.
For us, the permission for a nation to be brazen.
To buck progressiveness, and opt instead for the
reemergence of an old ethic, long thought to be gone
but merely buried, now excavated, with all of its soil
falling from its muscle and chest spread like a
revealing storm.

And so we marched, and gathered, and started
campaigns, and dedicated social media pages to
our cause, and created events, and signed petitions,
and called our congressmen, and manned phones.

I say *we*. Yet I barely dipped my toe into the movement
that had formed, a hearkening to the decade I was born
to, that most formidable of decades. The day of the very
first march — rich with pink knitted beanies and signs
that read "not up for grabs" — I was on the road to my
father's house, where he had taken a turn for the worse.
I crawled down the 5 Fwy at a trudge that betrayed my
frustrations with life, with timing, with passing Downtown
where history was being made, and I could nearly see it
in action from the distant cabin of my 4-wheel drive,
and I was not a part of it.

We took turns watching my father, making sure he
did not take a fall. Feeding him, dressing him, singing
to him, loving him. The open wound on his outer thigh
needed cleaning. His favorite pudding was now
despised. This was the movement I belonged to.
This was the history I was a part of making.
This was the mourning still on its way, imminent,
promised. Unconcerned with a nation's tide.

And we would survive it. We would transcend it.
We would awaken every morning, and re-fall in love
with the very idea of life. Even against the monstrous
shadow of its threat to leave us in the lurch.

The Steps Are Loose

or there are no steps. Everything, I instantly realize,
is going to be precarious from here on out. My ordered
life, my straight lines, my need for symmetry, are not
going to put this in a neat box for me to be able to

conceptualize, intellectualize, and buff up to acceptability.
Precarious from here on out. I am carrying a heavy bag.
Thank god it has handles. My little brother, carrying the
heavier, helps me down the steep embankment. And

damn it, I didn't wear the right shoes for this. Are there
right shoes for this? I've written about the homeless a
thousand times. The food in the bags we're carrying
smells delicious even to the nose of this full-bellied girl.

Christmas dinner already eaten, heads already bowed,
and the standard gratitude platitude for the *"food we are
about to receive"* already given. Once safely down the
embankment, careful of the loose steps, the ones

missing, broken, blunted with shards, and approaching
the undercarriage of the bridge, descending like
Orpheus, I can already sense the virtual city we are
about to broach. Breach? There is no door to knock

on. The idea of infiltrating someone's rightful home,
invited or uninvited, is muddy. Can't put it in a box, the
box I always need. To put things in. Yet home this is
to the plethora of off-the-grid people who belong to

a dubious club. I've written about the homeless a
thousand times. I realize (though this is our first time
doing this) that taking food to the homeless on
Christmas Day is a common practice among the

compassionate. We're a compassionate family,
but it has never dawned on us to do this, even though
I've written about this a thousand times.
Before seeing a soul, we hear his voice. "Mom!"

he calls out feverishly to our mother, amid the
hundreds. She is subdued today, to say the least.
Her son lives here, as of a week, or so, ago. Our
littler brother. It has never dawned on us to do this.

Where's the box for this? Where's his box?
How will he sleep tonight and stay warm? He cannot
come home [he says] because the world he knows is
not making sense. And the box for this remains empty.

I cannot fill it, because the world I know is not making
sense. Things not making sense seems to be the
only thread right now that connects us.
The steps are loose, or there are no steps.

In the Time Before Thought

I grazed voraciously
From the forests of
Rims ledges cliffs
Mowed down the terrain
With brazen ignorance and ample equilibrium
Singed the hems of statement and conviction with matches
And watched to see if whole fires would swell
Then thought came
Beautiful conscious thought
Selling me right
Selling me expectation
Selling me culture
And I cowered beneath
Between and within the folds of jealousy and fear
Gave no further trouble to the ministers of civility and predilection
Became polite
Thought taught me to fit into small spaces
How I miss the thoughtlessness of ripping holes in the fabric
Of being a witness to new worlds
Demolished and reinvented
Somewhat similar to ones past but always shifted
How I miss shifting
Singeing
Mowing and grazing until I am
Bloated and gross
How I miss not being polite

They Always Remind Me of Butterflies

I stand at our door with your heart

in my hand.

The mesmerizing Monarchs flit,

bounce and swarm.

Their voices, each, sing a pulsing

rhythm and grating harmony

that could challenge the master Penderecki

to a duel.

They land at our door, carry you away

on their backs, swallowed whole. Actually, not

whole; a heart no longer works

and is poking at death, as at a fireplace

of glowing logs.

Off the Monarchs fly, their wings of reddish gold,

flecked with black.

Black straps holding you to their breast,

carrying you away. Don't worry, my love, your heart

is with me, not the Monarchs.

I'll keep it safe while you convince them of your

aliveness, and tell them to deliver you home.

And I watch the Monarchs speed away,

erupting from each other

like flecks of paint flung by the

master Pollock's hand,

each with a piece of you inside,

and proceed to thin

their collective largeness to fragments

and abstracts,

even as their Penderecki chord lessens,

fades, and disappears.

A chord I will hear in every din and silence,

corner and copse,

until the day you return to me,

to collect your heart.

Equilibrium

Her dog was beaten by an uncle; a disciplinary measure.
"This is how you keep 'em in line, baby girl."
Her skinny child arms attempting to choke-hold the
bastard-with-the-belt
came to no avail.
And her sweet Cody Boy never trusted human touch again.
Dog now long gone. Bastard too.
Doesn't matter.
She carries it.
Her brow perpetually casts a shade over wide swaths of landscape,
offering no sun for growth, stunting life at every turn.

They called him nigger. Tortured him for sport.
The man who looked like her father,
her brothers,
her uncles.
He was somebody's somebody, until he wasn't.
A species endangered.
An unsurprising headline.
This is not 1955.   This is not 1955.
And it breaks her.
The swath of shade grows wider, stretches for miles.
She carries it.

His drunkenness wouldn't accept no. He called it lovemaking.
The pageant of firearms that adorned his display case like trophies
loomed and promised death if she didn't love him back.

That one's gone too; the drunkenness eventually got him.

Everything dies.

Doesn't matter.

She carries it.

And entire hemispheres are shaded.

She holds onto life till it cuts her hands.

Then she holds on tighter.

It isn't always this

precarious.

This need of a seatbelt.

This need for a crash helmet.

This need for Dramamine.

Sometimes

it is beautiful.

Gentle on the stomach.

Even radiant.

Sometimes uncles don't beat dogs.

Drunks don't rape.

Racists aren't.

And mothers shade their children.

But in wide swaths of fear

until there is no sun

and growth is stunted.

And treacheries are, merely for the moment, abated.

But sometimes life is beautiful.

And sunsets bleed horizons.

And food is not wasted
but is shared among the starving,
the great sea of starving that will never know a day of plenty,
while others will know nothing except cushion and warmth.
But sometimes life is beautiful!
And children are not sold into slavery and made into soldiers
before their first ejaculation.
They are allowed to play and climb and chase their dogs,
which are not beaten by bastards
who rape and taunt and turn children into killing machines.
And she understands AA.
And she understands religion.
And she understands drugs.
And she understands violence.
And sometimes life is beautiful.
Even radiant.
And grips can be loosened.
And blood need only signify womanhood.
And oxygen can be breathed and not restricted by the
looming shadow of display cases.
Sometimes she thinks about breathing.
Sometimes she just breathes.
Sometimes breath.
And breath is
golden.

Inflammation

He loves his brother.

Admires his brother's beauty in a way that is almost unnerving.

He wants that kind of beauty to wear on his own body.

He longs for the looks women give his brother constantly, who has no trouble finding love.

No one ever looks at him that way.

Is it because he lights the world with matches, pumping gasoline from his pores, and women want a smooth-talker?

Or is it because he can't harmonize *his* world and the *world's* world, and his brother just seems to sing through it — whoever's world — with a grace he painfully covets.

His brother's effortless life rills over his hands like too-hot water from a faucet because the pipes are baking in one-hundred-degree weather.

Unexpected and injurious.

Requiring a yanking away.

He just wants to love someone, and be loved.

Like, lay-her-down-on-the-hard-concrete kind of love, where you don't care that your skin is sanded and your bones are chalked and the elements are charging and the authorities are taking you away in cuffs because this

isn't acceptable public behavior, but you don't care, and she doesn't care, and the world is envious of your love.

He just wants tenderness.

Not the kind that comes from an inflamed sore when touched.

But the kind that needs touches, is salved by touches.

The kind that softens sand.

Woodwork

No one oohhs and ahhhs
the kid who does well
in school gets a job makes
a career takes care of his
folks finds love lives in the
world mastering the art of
harmony

They save all their awe and
efforts for the kid who fell
who got dealt a bad hand
by god by fate by eating too
much sugar by loneliness
and pain

There is no room for normal
at this party be broken or else
get lost in the drapes
the sea foam that buries the
trees that speak and shade

Take the kid for granted
know he is all right and can
stand on his two feet and
wield an answer with

breathtaking clarity and
insight take comfort that
his answers his embracing
arms his solid wisdom will
always serve and save all
your awe for the Christ
figure taking over the
breadth of the sky casting
wide blankets of shade
across the world promising
greatness

Matte is more fused with
stable matter than gloss
but not nearly as
mesmerizing

This is the affliction of the
kid who does well in school
gets a job makes a career
takes care of his folks
finds love lives in the world
and masters the art of
harmony

Is There Room For Me Here?

Can you accommodate the eye

in the middle of my face?

(symbol of enlightenment or monstrous gorgon, you decide)

The legs that crawled from Christianity to Eastern thought?

The terrain treacherous but called?

The knees that scraped and gashed themselves

on the cold ground from the desperate

worship of elysian stardust?

The unforgiving fissures created between

black and white, whole and broken, where I live,

like a pestilent insect writhing, crushed,

as the closing walls begin to seal the cracks forever?

Revived, if not exactly repaired?

For, there can be no room, no room at all, for leaks

in faith.   In hope.   In love.

I've been known to leak a little.

Om gam ganapataye namaha

I am impelled daily to intone.

Is there even room for me here?

Dancing

I am staring into

the space

between two eyes.

Father on

one side of me

brother on the

other. A pair of

diagnoses

A pair of

beauties.

Father no longer

has conversation.

He gestures at things

in the air. Painting

perhaps? He was

magnificent

in his day.

Brother has

too much

conversation.

Finding his way

in that open

realm before

linear thought.

Dancing

both

untethered.

Children

There's the time my father told my kid brother and me that we
owned an airplane, and he pointed one out as we passed the
town airfield that housed private Cessnas. Our big sister rolled

eyes and apparently got on my father later for telling us big bold
lies. What possible purpose could that serve? And my father
just chuckled, and loved our wide-eyed-ness that WE OWNED

A PLANE! Big sis knew she was talking to just another kid. She'd
have to be the grownup here. Here's the thing: Sometimes it
was Daddy who was more kid than us. Sometimes it was Mom,

who was fond of reliving her cheerleading days for us, her rapt
audience. And rapt we were. We had a cheerleader mom, a
fabricator dad, and a sister often called on to be parent. And

never because ours didn't know how. But because in addition to
life lessons, moral guidance, and food on the table, a wide berth
for flights of fancy was absolutely required. When my father

remarried and sired two more children, decades younger than
us, they would grow up to have their own childhood tales of their
Peter Pan dad. Yet we all came together. Not one generation

and another. Not this camp and that. We were one body. My
father's children. We linked arms in a chain that never once broke.
Not even when troubles brewed, or someone got lost. Today we

are all adults, yet will forever be our parents' children. And the
relativity of that word is intensely comforting, as if a respite from the
noxious tyranny of grownup things. Something my parents knew well.

Salt & Silt

Every week is the task of emptying my mailbox
Every week not every day
The Great Avoider my only coping companion
& the mailbox has become the gateway to
untold disquiet   Not even paychecks that show up
to help alleviate a main character in my anxieties
or sweet greetings from long lost friends
& wonderful sisters
can dissociate my brain from the clutches
of groping fingers that daily claw at my throat
claw at my thin purse
claw at my usually thwarted efforts to erect legacy for myself
claw at my need for consistency & serenity & for
no one else to die or go off their meds.

No matter how much good news also flows the mailbox river
it will still go unattended for days, years, until its content
is saturated, waterlogged, & ultimately downed
to the river's mossy bed collecting in miles & miles of silken clumps
to the discovery of pirates & priests centuries from now
when the earth is finally bled dry of replenishment
All rivers & oceans vanquished
& the billions of piles of salt & silt
hardened into papier-mâché mountains
whose ghosts once lived & struggled with caught breath most days
give perhaps a clue or maybe not
Maybe only just a Stonehenge-like mystical fascination
without ever a hint of the stifled bones crumbled to powder
that lurk within.

His Hands

While massaging my
father's hands,
I tell him how
beautiful they are, and
remind him of the
artist he is, and of
the miracles on canvas,
hundreds of times
over, that those artist's hands
have created.
He seems pleased to hear this, though
he has no recollection of
having been an artist.
His diagnosis has largely
locked him away
from us, though periodically I see
those hands motion in the air,
like a dancer's,
and I wonder,
"Is he painting?"
The art that may well still tug
at him,
even as he travels the
abstract realms of dementia,
must be something
to behold.

My Superior Beast

She is hanging on, distressed and in pain. A pain she will
never let me see, though it is apparent beyond her skills at
pokerfacing. I don't know whether it's better to tell her that
it's okay to let go, or to be her pep squad and root her on to

keeping living. One thought I've had is that she is hanging
on for me.   I show her my sadness, and maybe I shouldn't.
I want her to rail against death with everything she has,
because it's what we do. We deny, we revolt, we go kicking

and screaming. We fear and loathe the very idea. Animals
don't operate that way. They are more innate survivors than
we are when threatened by the unnatural dangers designed
to take them out early. But when it's their natural time to

go, organs shutting down, step by arduous step, they are
far more plugged into the cycles of life than humans will
ever be. We are the inferior beasts. She has stopped eating.
I cannot entice this ordinarily always-voracious beauty to

take a bite of food, to save my life.   She is trying to tell me,
"I'm ready. Let me do what I have to do." And I am trying
my damnedest to be her cheerleader, because we've had
sixteen years together. And while all I want to do is piss

and rail, the word she continually shows me is *grace*.
She purrs until her last breath. My hand on her wraithlike
torso feels her heart stop. Have I been a good mom? I
have some inkling now of the affliction my friends who

are parents go through. The constant worry for their
children's wellbeing.   The constant wonder of their own
merits as caregivers. It has to be a love/hate thing, the
debilitating worry, on top of worry, on top of worry.

At this moment I am hating it. I have never experienced
parturition, nor will, over which some have challenged
the wholeness of my womanhood.
But I have bled as much from the hole torn from my

heart as I can imagine bearing. My girl is gone now.
I never do learn the art of letting her go. And me being
devastated is, in a sense, and in the face of the choice
to be childless, a strange assurance of my goodness.

Duck & Weave

While hiking a beautiful wilderness trail

on the morning the news breaks about the

"mother of all bombs"

the magnificent white-tailed buck & I,

upon our encounter,

freeze,

lock eyes,

gear haunches,

bramble & sky between us,

each silently cautioning the other.

As the antlered gent prances away toward the hills

with a grace beyond my ability for words,

I see the common dance

we share.

An understanding.

Both move

in the zigzag manner

that maneuvers

the land mines,

bear traps

& treacherous terrain

of our respective lifescapes.

For him, the wily beasts of prey.

For me, a preening America.

A Morning Cup

A fly in the room assaults the morning stillness.
I am annoyed by its usurping though I wouldn't
mind the playful romp of my fur girl right now.

I still feel her here,
months after she's left me.

Coffee percolates rhythmically.
In it — I hear song.

Soon my father's absence will be the
presence I'll feel.

He's only been here once
to the new space. What I know is
that it'll never happen again, as the
stairs were his treachery.

And the need I have for that single visit to be enough
to keep some part of him in this room after he's gone,

and for the flicker of lights to

reassure that they do come back,

they visit,

they burrow deep,

to forgive us our transgressions,

to join us for a morning cup,

is a compelling one.

As compelling as the smudging of white sage

whose cedary stench collects in the corners

of a house that believes in magic.

Wait

In you
light
lives.

Not to be
mowed down

yet
neither
free to
bloom.

In the eaves
of the broken,
light struggles,
refracting only
in shards

misshapen
& distorted

but not mowed
not moved
not silenced.

Navigating the
murky oceans,
strained & treacherous,
your purity nearly
trampled,
limbs reach
for a messenger.

My love cries
for one
you can
hear.

Send him a messenger he can hear.

In you
the battle
wages
between light
and loss

for
your place
in the world.

Are you
answering
the call
of your own
truth,
or have you
been
hijacked?

Be still, child.
Be still
and wait;
It is coming.

And while you wait,
use my love
to parry
thieves,

to keep your light
safe.
Use my love
to harbor.

Use my love.
It can take it.

And wait.

In This Room

That I am the one
alone with my father at
his moment is purely chance.

It is 4:14 am, and the house is quiet. Though we're all
here, this moment leaves me alone with my father, who
will die tonight; it's just a matter of when. I have had
some developing anxiety lately. I've often felt that it's

as embarrassingly elementary as: We get what we
deserve. Period. And after a lifetime of missteps and
regret I feel fairly certain that I am destined to die in a
heinous car crash for all my sins. As a result, I've lately

been fearful of cars. Getting behind the wheel of them.
Being a passenger in them. Encountering them and their
owners on the most manic freeways in the world (yes, you,
Los Angeles). So I almost didn't make it. I paused as I got

the call from home that my father was beginning his
transition. I was sixty miles away. My heart raced; I
should be there and nowhere else. But I paused. I paused
again when the second phone call from my brother revealed

that he was only minutes away from arriving at Dad's.
So, there's just me, then? Who won't be there when Dad

passes, out of this life? Only me? While everyone else
rallies, because rally is what you do. I guess that was

the one that unpaused me. I strapped on guile — an
ill-fitting dress — and got on those deathtrap freeways.
The way I came to see it, as I drove, with extreme
paranoia about every auto that seemed to be inching

into me, was that if it's my time to go, in the most fiery,
bloody way one can imagine, that would still be better
than living the remainder of my life in the self-hatred that
I would choose cowardice and PTSD-level anxiety over the

privilege of holding my father's hand as he completes his
extraordinary task on this earth. So here I am, at 4:14 a.m.,
and our entire life together as father and daughter floods
the corners of my eyes. We're all here, floating in and out

of his room over the course of several hours, several days,
holding vigil, being here as much for each other as for him.
My stepmother, especially, has been the most solid rock I've
ever witnessed. She's not indulging her irrational fears.

> That I am the one
> alone with my father at
> his moment is purely chance.
> Except what if it isn't?

What if, of all his children to see him over the threshold
(there are five of us), he chooses the one most fragile?
It could be argued that a younger brother who wrestles
with a Bipolar Disorder diagnosis is the fragile one.

At least, in that invincible, God-complex universe that is
my brother's, he is absolutely certain of his power and
worth. Of course, only in my own troubled universe can
there even be an "at least" regarding a brother's diagnosis.

I am bitterly aware. But what if my father is saying to
me, at 4:14 a.m., through his shroud of unconsciousness,
his sheer drape between this life and another: "Darling
daughter, the rest of my children are good in the world.

They have learned their worth. You have been struggling
for fifteen years. Ever since the estrangement with your
mother at the time of her death. You have self-flagellated
in the most dramatic ways, because she died alone and

you hold yourself responsible for every bit of it. Darling
girl, see me out. Hold my hand, and sing to me. Though
my eyes are closed, and my breath is thready, I am listening
and holding your hand too. You. See me out. So that you

can be atoned. So that you can cancel out regret. So that,
against your fears, too closely linked to annihilation, you

can stop looking, almost begging, to meet the eyes of
road-ragers and challenge them to take you out."

My God, what if?

The throng has been his vigil all night. Yet at 4:15 a.m. on
a Thursday, the dark hours of morning, a daughter alone,
holding her father's hand, he takes his last breath. I watch
for his chest to rise one more time. An almost violent stare.

It never does. My father's youngest walks in the room, takes
our father's hand, and confirms the death that I have been
staring at these vast seconds. We hold each other at
his bedside, as the rest of my family enters and gathers.

And we feel the enormous heft of siblinghood, marriage,
fatherhood, all bound together in this room by my
father's very sinews. It is the most precious moment
I can imagine. We all feel this. We are in sync. A family.

As for *our* moment, father and daughter alone, it will
be forever mine that until, and perhaps even inside
of, his very last breath, my father was still taking
care of his child. Offering her peace.

Should she choose to accept it.

Harbored

is the

urn

that

contains

the

powdery

alchemy

of my

mother's

blood

&

bones.

Are her

hurts

in there

too?

Or have they

been

mercifully

charred

into

oblivion?

Splinters

I called my mother minutes after the twin towers fell. I expected a solidarity with her, a mutual oh-my-godding we could share. To bond in that instant of a nation under siege. Still so fresh that we didn't know if L.A. might be next. Her response sounded disconnected. And I realized that her struggles had reached a zenith, and nothing else in the world mattered. I wish I'd called my father first. He was an emotional animal who felt tragedies deeply. He and I could've mourned together.

I called my father minutes after the first Black man in America's history was elected to the highest office. I expected a solidarity with him, a mutual 'bout-time jubilant cry; that we had actually lived to witness this making of history. His response sounded disconnected. Almost "what's the big deal?" And I realized that he had never much been involved with the Civil Rights Movement. He was a man who stayed close to home, kept his head down to do his work and raise his family. I wish I'd had my mother to call. She — who had done the lunch counter sit-ins for voter rights, and carried picket signs, and marched — had passed away six years before the man with the very African name became our 44th president, never getting to have that moment in her lifetime. She and I could've praised together.

Tribulation

&

the floods

of houston

were biblical

&

the cali

wildfires

said to be

seen from

space.

in the first year

of the new

presidency

a declaration

of end

times was the

easy joke

luscious even.

a way to

find some

righteousness

in our pain

to

seek refuge

in the

comforting

mythology

of good

&

evil.

Things Known

Your ribs ache where
they punch you
repeatedly.
You don't mean
to disturb the peace.
You are trying to
reconcile the world
outside and in.

Inside
feels alive and invincible.
You don't believe
you can die.
Is that the reason you
keep letting them
beat you?
To show them your
impenetrable Zen?
Your love is unconditional
even in the face
of your face
being bashed because
you just won't

leave people alone,

wishing only to

show them your kindness

and share your discoveries.

You speak of lofty things.

Of God.

Of the illusion of separation

and that we are all one.

The rhetoric of sages.

All while begging for

cigarettes.

Outside

is where rules are followed

and civil understandings make

for a society

that runs with some

measure of

efficiency

and jobs are worked

and money is made

so that life can

be maintained.

You shun all of that.

It is beneath

humanity's greater purpose

and only belongs to the small-minded.

The limited.

And you are limitless.

Are you lonely there?

In that space where

you are invincible

and unreachable

and saving the world

all alone

because

the rest of us have

not yet arrived?

Or are *we*?

Our Kodachrome Life

The names that Sister gave us
upon her return from Africa to the
    tiny world we knew
were ancient and mystical as sea glass
       Crowns too big for our little heads
but we wore them anyway with lifted chests
    — Kelele, Kuamini — little brother, little
          sister — noisemaker, believer — till the crowns
    slipped straight down over our
dirty faces and grubby play clothes like hula hoops
    And she carried us
        across rivers and
    muddy banks
         from toys to poise
    bare feet sloshing
     Today laughter
reverberates like ghosts
   throughout childhoods revisited
Pinky swears and blood oaths   Colonel Mustard in the
       parlour with the candlestick
And the cracks in the orange vinyl patio chairs
     And the homemade monkey bread
(sometimes a rival batch between our mother and father's
culinary prowess and playfully competitive natures)
   And our sister's delicious enchantments aimed
       at empowering us long before we had any clue of it
     And the kodachrome-colored gels to light our Christmas tree
       to light our way
         are what I remember most

Silence

We're born
We die
And in between we try
to conquer the road the lash the lie the crash

We love
We seek
We float between the meek
and massive erosion of the spirit our will to clear it

We fall
We shout
We fight against the drought
the withered earth the rock the crumb the all the some

We lose
We rise
We have so many whys
We pose the questions to our peace our rod our selves our god

We kill
We eat
Watch history repeat
We lose allegiance with the stars our *objets d'art*

Where once was dirt

now is paved

The old road we've hungrily craved

is gone is lost is tempest-tossed

a tart burlesque

an arabesque

and then the rest

Reaching Ears

When I think of what I consider lost

that you cry "found!"

my hands begin to hurt.

Indigenous cultures do not

medicalize antisocial behavior.

They say… what if mental disorders never existed.

A society may name its codes of conduct,

but we are under no obligation to adhere.

The indigenous say this does not mean a fall;

instead, a shamanistic vocation

might well be the call.

A call one's tribe will never understand.

And so, the one must pull away from the tribe

for robes to be taken.

This you have seized upon with cunning and brilliance.

Indigenous peoples have suffered horrifically

at the hands of "corrected" societies forever,

so this position is unsurprising

in its breathtaking rebellion.

It *is* breathtaking.

Even compelling.

When I think of what I consider lost

that you cry found,

my hands hurt, and shoulder-blades follow.

Do your hands hurt as mine do?

As each pair attempts to hold opposing birds

in their palms, and bid them sing?

Each of us depends on ours to out-sing the other.

To wrest hearts from chests.

Instead, they squawk and screech violently.

Peck out eyes. Upset order.

Upset innocents.

The universe created has resembled

not so much the healing fields of the shaman

as a dog-fighting ring.

Will you ever come home?

Or is home, for you,

yet another call to answer,

another search for higher agreement,

another set of robes to take,

another bird that sings,

in the hope of reaching ears?

SATC Moment

Today I saw an old episode
of *Sex and the City* where the girls talk about
those shameful things they do when they're home

alone that they would be mortified
being caught at. When I saw that episode I
sat forward in my chair thinking, wow,

this show's about to go THERE! Portray
some actual pathos and internal struggle.
How awesome! They're about to say, "you're

not alone, crazy people!   We get
you! We're representing you, and writing you with
insight and humor!" And I will feel

not so alone. But gotten. And then
Carrie says something like: I eat crackers standing
up over the sink reading fashion

magazines. Followed by Miranda
sharing: I wear Borghese gloves while watching soaps.
This is their nascent notion of Dark

Recesses territory. Cute-drunk
trifles decked in Manolo Blahniks. And in that
instant, I know unequivoc'ly

that pop entertainment is nowhere
near ready to take us to the pitch of the caves,
the ones Campbell assures us of. And

once again I am alone. And scorned.
And judged. Because I'm not quick-witted, and glib, and
clever. Not living my life in a

Michael Patrick King comedy, as
much as I dream every day of doing so. I
live in the caves. Where nothing is sleek,

but porous and absorptive. Where the
darkly vast abyss beckons the tormented to
seek the answers to life if they dare.

And bravery is tested. And the
thickness of marrow reigns. And the dampish walls drip
the sweat of longing and belonging.

Penumbra

An Intervention Staged by the
3 Fates for their Little Girl

Your clothes don't quite fit   Do they   Little Pearl?

Your child bones beat drums   A tribal warning to the others

You sprout talons that rip your flesh & let your blood

but they serve you well enough

Winter sees you when spring does not but spring receives all your

love unrequited

& still you beg

You strap on limbs & latch them with buckles to parry knives

Grow blades of your own when limbs fail

You & us forever kid   we always promise

Yet we've had to leave you & your foolishness a time or two

Since when do you wish for blond hair?

We have done our best to drape you in asafetida bags

Running off all prospects for love due to the stink

just to protect you from predators

Who is protecting everyone else from you?

We wish blackness for you   we wish blood

You rise   But sideways

Kick open doors so violently that they hit the walls &

slam back your way

A keystone cops bit played to exhaustion & bloodied foreheads

Music is the moon for you   Little Pearl

It sings when bones are broken & wits are snapped

making oceans gust

making a glue to put you back together   If temporary

Your bones outgrow their flesh with each fix

& you seem to be trying your damnedest to fry your own lungs

with a magnifying glass

Yet you give birth

relentlessly

rending garments & offspring with

equal release equal multiplying explosions of fantasia

Escaping in flight yet always skysick

The sea rises

burying touches that lead to love

The sea rises

burying touches that never lead to love

The sea rises

& you have stayed down there too long without air

A bluing apparition catching & shrieking as your creature soars up

holding its own against gargoyles only ever just in the nick of time

Your hair draws tight from the seawater

So tight   So dense

A wild nappy black jungling of bramble & bergamot & beasty things

I have a particular gift for taming the wild

but you never let me near

says Fate #1

The 1 who breastfeeds you

I think you want whole angel oaks to sprout from your tiny head

to give you crown & spread

says the 1 who calls herself sister

to wrap tentacles around us all like tumors strangling organs

says the 1 enlisted from the future   A clue that childhood will be

survived and adulthood will carry its lessons like jewels

You fear earwax on washcloths & breath on your neck
but have managed to find your ballast against the worst of it
through marvelous birth that you give time & time again
melting mountains searing rivers quaking earth but never quite
scraping gum
You look for heroes in hopscotch squares & kitchen cupboards
& Tarot's fool

When scratched-off epidermis covers your mattress like
confetti & only haze & copper droplets adorn your oatmeal pallor
& sour hide is trapped between nail bed & nails
you rise from its heap of eczematic flakes like the phoenix we keep
telling them you are

How many times have you died before our eyes?

The drowning   The strangling   The stoning   The stare

Still you rise

Imperceptible to everyone but us

& winter

We see you   Little Pearl

We have tried to teach you a few things & you have been

nearly unteachable

Winter was more successful with her lessons

but time eventually gave way to understanding   All you needed

was our patience

& we need yours

For we have never quite gotten the hang

of your sorcery

Frankly we're afraid to learn

Think a thought & bring them all down   Little Pearl

That's always been your way

Is it still?

Rather than the thousand petals opening a lotus

of boundlessness & grace

you have danced 10,000 thorny sphincter-tight rosebuds &

blue babies & floods behind your eyes

commandeered the deliverance of your own Armageddon

via your lacewing army

That's what they call you

Lacewing   Stinkfly

& you answer

& you answer

They have never regarded you except to deride

when all you did was arrive YOU

Yet you insist on feeding the beasts

This is where we lose our patience with you   Little Pearl

That time you cracked your skull

a genuine accident

not the locusts coming after you

though because of precedent

you claimed it & forever mastered victimhood

we tended your head with balms

Hoping some would penetrate beyond the fracture

Hoping for a baptism if not an exorcism

We're not certain our efforts have ever worked
but we will say this
When you give birth   Little Pearl
time & time again   O Little Pearl   Our Little Pearl
this is when your alchemy works
This is when the world gets fatter from your touch
From your mining of color & planets
From the music sung to you by the moon
You fatten too   You fatten with sun
You fatten till talons turn to wings
which always takes its toll on your back
The in & the out of it
The way up & the fall down
But up is always just around the corner again
So don't be beaten   Little Pearl
No matter their design

Stop knocking your teeth against the table-end
for the tooth fairy   She only gives a quarter
Hold out for more before you determine to bleed

This is our prayer for you   Little Pearl

Keep seeking the bead of light

the refraction of it off your wings

Keep catching it in mason jars

like lightning bugs

You prefer to call them fireflies

Our prayer for you is lightning bugs

You & us forever kid

Maybe someday we can stop leaving you

Elegy for the One More

It wasn't a struggle.

He didn't gasp or choke or moan.

He took a breath,

not unlike every other

for nearly a century,

and then there

were no more.

I waited.

There'd been gaps before,

sometimes as

long as twenty-five seconds,

and suddenly he would inhale again.

Not this time.

And it wasn't auspicious.

Simply absent.

Had I known this was his last breath,

I might've sung to him as he was taking it.

He always loved that I was a singer.

We loved singing together.

Even in the last days,

when he had no more language in him,

he had song.

But it didn't dawn on me to sing.

I realize now that I just

genuinely believed

he had one more breath in him.

I wonder how long it will be before

I stop waiting for it.

Notes

I used to be confident about my
voice. I could stand on a stage, and open my mouth,
and mastery was effortlessly mine.

While everyone else was belting out bold
notes, fat with blaze and bullet-train verve, I simmered
in pure tones, unfettered by frippery

and the need for worship. I was a Zen
marksman, shooting only when the aim was science,
and the kill utterly guaranteed and

firmly in sight. Others blasted messy
gunfire, spewing melismatic gunpowder,
dusting the air with a beguiling fog,

requiring protective goggles. Me, I
was buoyant. Stripped. Unafraid to be unadorned.
No need to hit the highest notes, the death

defying notes, the longest notes, applause
engendering notes. I could slay them with far less,
and I knew it. The astonishing notes

eluded me anyway. Dazzle was
never mine. I had dirt, soil, roots. I could grow a
field of hawthorn without batting an eye.

Today I push. Cannot find the sweet spot.
"Time is never kind," they say, and say, and say, and...
Today I'm afraid the note won't be there,

a lover I can count on. But will be
shot through with raggedy tread, with loss, with pain. So
I hold back. Trill and tremble. White-knuckle.

Clamp down and suffocate it just a bit,
until it ekes out, a fraction of the brazen
soldier it used to be. Or I go the

other way. Blast it out. Obliterate
the air around me with a perilous sky fall.
More batshit than brazen. I never thought

I would stoop to this, cower behind an
ocean of notes to mask my uncertainty. Now
I am a belter just like all the rest.

Pulling out every stop. Not because I
love the ostentation — I do not — but because
nuance left me for a younger woman.

Pull

We laugh at the silliest things.

Pulling memories like taffy.

His laugh, our father's laugh.

We pull and pull.

His walk, our father's walk.

Wrap taffy like winter coats around our whole bodies,

and lap up the sweetness of memory.

His brow, our father's sweat.

His history, our father's making.

They once ganged up on me.

The torture my brother endured

at my big-sister hands,

I was warned against by my father.

One of these days, he'll be big enough

not to take it anymore, and then

you'll be sorry.

Not even the decency to be politically correct

and take no sides.

The boys, I called them. Even as a kid.

Now one of them has left us.

And the other?

His laugh, our father's laugh.

Music I'll hold inside my winter coat of taffy forever.

Sing

I don't know
that I've ever truly
gotten inside
your pain

You have tended to make
yourself so small
when I have seen you
only as giant
With arms tucking
around our hearts
to shelter us teach us

You tuck yourself too
But with a different promise
I have seen the dance for years
An almost curtsy

Holy is this music
of a sister whose voice
has found itself
after all the years of
serving others'
All the years of being moon to our suns
All the years of a
stubborn laryngitis
And finally sings

Joon

She scoops earth into her hands

Makes alchemy in her garden

Draws out the stems from their roots

The same way she draws

connection out of her Love

when all other is severed

The same way she sees God

in her Firstborn's ravings

nonetheless angling

for shift

The same way she cradles

his head her head all the heads of all her loves

Lives for our wellness and comfort

Calls each of us *joon*

An endearment from her culture

The same way she fights for her loves

Scraps dirty and risks death if she must

Draws out the stems from their roots

Till bulb becomes flower

and pain becomes power

Him

He's been gone

maybe an hour now.

We call it gone,

we say gone,

yet in moments of collapse

one of us runs over to him,

scoops him up in cradling arms,

and tells him how much

we love him.

Another of us gets it right, observing:

"Isn't it funny how we do that?

Talk to him? He is not that body.

Yet we cling to flesh."

His youngest is sometimes his wisest.

We are urged to touch him,

to see.

Even now I can't keep

from calling this hollow body,

this marble sculpture,

this passing experience,

which nevertheless has

cracked our very world,

him.

Uninvited

you have stayed too long
you have settled in the space
that belongs to someone else

fastened your ties around
my bones to move them
in a certain way

with a certain sway
erected a shroud around me
to shelter the delicates

that were never delicate
until you came to visit
with your contract and a pen

an oath of transience
a taunt that the road
leading out is tricked with

booby traps and banana peels
and no such promise of wisdom
as the legends like to tell it

the earth existed for
four point five billion years
before I showed up

will I really have even been here?
there is only the stuff
built with my hands as evidence of my life

and even that will erode
and disintegrate in a blink
take on the same uninvited guest

the one that eats us
out of house and home
leaving only ash

Concerto for Breath and Orchestra

May I just lie here?

Let time pass?

Not move my bones one inch

but allow the dust to settle in my corners

and watch the world whiz by

faster than it's ever whizzed before?

Do I have permission to be exhausted?

Does the world's preoccupation with fame

as the barometer for a valuable life need to

have its claws perpetually in my nape?

Will the things that my hands have created

cease to have meaning if they don't

change the world?

They change *my* world daily.

My father—the artist—never sought acclaim.

He did the most crucial thing he

could do.

He made art.

Today I float on my back in a shallow pool

with my ears immersed.

Stare up at the trees that blow in the wind.

I cannot hear a thing

beyond my own

submarine breath.

Just the way I need it for a bit.

Profound in its echoey EQ,

slowed down to a pulse

that mesmerizes me

like a good ommmmm track.

It slows the trees down too,

whose windsways

are a sultry hula.

The world is beautiful

right now.

All I want is to be an observer.

Take in these moments

and cry at them.

Maybe put them into words.

Maybe not.

I want to no longer

have agenda,

give chase,

need cred.

Do I still need cred?

After years at it?

What does the cred even mean?

And why is cred's shortened,

lazy version of an

actual word

suddenly so absurd to me?

I laugh at the

Cool Daddio stink

it has to it.

We all talked that way for years.

The world is absurd to me.

Absurd and beautiful.

And I grow queasy constantly trying to

decide which ride I'm on,

because absurd can be fun.

But today I just want to lie here.

Unabsurd.

Unironic.

Underwater.

Swaddled in amniotic azure.

A witness to the

silent

windswayed

trees.

Just the way I need it for a bit.

A moment

without the constant siren

of a family in peril.

And breath that

reverberates

throughout my

underwater ears,

in concert

with birds and

fault lines

and fathoms.

And time that stops

splendidly

for just an

instant.

A Talk with Death

heather heyer
lost her life
two days after
my father lost his

while he slept the peaceful
final sleep of a life that had
been long & cultivated
quietly with purpose

she was raged out of hers
too short too grim
purpose coursing even more
forcefully than her blood

nIne days after that
the moon passed across the sun
its corona visible through
7-eleven eclipse glasses
darkness falling for an instant
before the penumbra graduated
to light again
startling symbol of promised flux

& no matter the conversation
the meaning in all of it still
stubbornly insisted itself
upon me

But There

High up on a mountain
Sun on my head
Easy to say thank you

Deep in the valley
Earth's shadow rising up against
shoulders
The cold shade of trials bearing
gravely upon me
A little harder

The light wants to hide
peek
wink
flood like shards through crevices
then skitter away
Wants to be fickle
Play at vanishing
but there

Harder to bathe in
its blanket of warmth
but there

Harder to see four feet
in front of me
but there

Playing coy
Its job not merely
to give of its brilliance and sheen
but to tease me with its
seeming dearth
A test of my resolve
Of my commitment to
glean the kernel anyway

Nature After All

What I never saw coming was the way in which it would become something I would crave the way one craves coffee. Runners talk about the runner's high. That has never been me. But I crave this.

Part crest, overlooking wide sweeps of mountain. Part enchanted forest, taking one into the bowels of nature with trees bridging overhead creating a canopy of shadow and mood. It sits on the northern tip of the valley and has become my sacred space. Sometimes there are horses on the trail, jackrabbits, the odd rattler. There is a symphony of frogs that are never seen but clearly surrounding me. And except for the concert of critters it is quiet. In all the years, there were never brooks; only gullies to suggest them. Then the rains came. And we saw colors we've never seen.

It has begun the cracking open of my heart in ways that have surprised me: Communing with creatures beyond pets and other humans, listening to their concert, moving among the ancient trees that drip their wisdom like sap, offering baptism (read Hesse's meditation on trees sometime...). It has brought me to a place I can manage when life throws its darts. I've been ducking and weaving the darts for nearly a year now. This seems the only place darts can't find me.

The trail has tweaked my receptor paradigm. Not only are the darts not present here, but I actually feel myself worthy of receiving blessings. Perhaps for the first time ever. The thing I am only just beginning to know is that blessings are flying all around me like gnats, and are in everything that happens to me. Yes, even in this Year of the Darts. It's all a bit of New Age rhetoric, which I pretend to fight like the plague. But I can't ignore the gnats. And why do I want to? It is nature, after all.

I have come to need this ritual so much lately, and the heart that it is beginning to fashion, that the first time I see graffiti on a tree I bristle horribly, wondering who would do such a thing. Can it hurt the tree? Or will the offended bark simply slough off over time? I start to envision what the perpetrator looks like. Probably a teenager. I continue to walk but remain disgusted, shaking my head visibly just in case I have an audience with any of the other hikers who might like to join me in a moment of righteous indignation: *"We can't have anything nice, can we?"*

On another occasion, the wonderful swing, really just a plank suspended by a sturdy rope hanging from one of

the masterful trees, like something out of Steinbeck,
and which I discovered my first week on the trail, is
suddenly there no more. The day I first discovered the
swing, it had been such a serendipitous moment that I
ran to it, grabbed hold, climbed on, swung around for a few
minutes, then leapt off, grinning like the Cheshire Cat for
that unplanned moment of letting loose my inner child.

She needs a lot of letting loose.

So when I see it broken, just a lone rope hanging with
no plank anywhere to be seen, I once again bristle,
once again envision the culprit, likely some unruly kid
without parental supervision. My judgments always
default to the young.

A brush fire threatens my beautiful canyon. I am actually
on the crest when the smell of forest fire and the
increasing brown sky run everyone out. I hasten home,
turn on the TV, and watch the fire burn not far, fearing it
will decimate my canyon. My father used to describe
strong structures as having "good bones," and I pray my
sacred space has good ones. I wonder where I'll go
instead if it's gutted, or if I'll just throw hands up and be

done with this nature ritual forever, defeated.

Ditto the natural gas leak that goes on and on, and keeps us all away, for an astonishing four months, the worst natural gas leak in U.S. history. I am not overly fond of hysterical hyperbole to describe my sacred space, almost as much as I'm not fond of environmental calamities that seep through bureaucratic cracks, no pun or politics intended. But damn it.

Then a friend, whom I one day take with me on the trail, actually dares to fall in love with it as gustily as I have, and starts going regularly himself.

This is my space.
   Sacred.
      Mine.

I will do whatever it takes to possess it. Whatever it takes to ignore the tenets of non-attachment that I have been taught in my dharma studies. Of letting go of expectations, of ownership. I will become a hoarder.
I have become a hoarder.
I am a hoarder.

The further shaping of my knotty little demons is in full

swing. I shake head, and sigh, and am dog-tired when
I recognize the blackening in my huffing and puffing and
stomping feet and jutting lower lip over having to share.
My judgments always default to the young.

This friend, who has had recent health challenges,
has been renewed by this ritual. I can't ignore that.
Why am I so hell-bent on doing so? And as I think on
those challenges, dire even, I find myself speaking
to a God I barely acknowledge like old marrieds sick
of each other's breathing: *Can you leave no one alone?*

The trail belongs to my friend. It belongs to the woman
walking her dogs. To the pair of lovers looking for a
secret bush behind which to do those luscious things
they do.
        (when did I get lonely?)
To the jogger getting fit. To the homeless man seeking
sanctuary from authorities.
        (stay, brother, please)
To the graffiti tagger who has a history I know nothing
of. The trail can take it. The trail is hearty. I'm not.
But the trail is. Hearty enough to withstand brush fires,
gas leaks, and the brattish impetuosity of someone
much too old to be a brat. The trail bounces back.

It is nature, after all.

I am constantly stricken by how easy it is — *maybe*
even a little irresistible? — to clamp down, bear the armor
of hurt, be the suffering martyr, garner the quiet awe of
others, sit high on my throne of reactivity, because
maybe I have no clue who I am without my wounds.

What I never saw coming was the way in which it
would perform the crucial surgery that this body has
needed, and crank open this heart. As with any
surgery, recovery is always the hardest part.

Along with the unexpected spring rains, and the gullies
now filled with babbling brooks, and colors I thought I'd
never see, not in this town, comes a kid with a spray paint
can in his hand and some mischief in his heart, who gawks
at the walking lady with her greedy "mine, mine!" face on,
and judges her for all the stuff she has yet to learn
about letting go.

It is nature, after all.

Knotty Little Demon

I romanticize the artist in my father

Choose at times to ignore that he found a niche

A niche that largely abated struggle and suffering

(touchstone of the artist, after all)

His niche was industry   was science

An artist in a scientist's world

Did he ever feel alien

He was damned gifted   He could be enthralling

He never had Van Gogh's torment

Picasso's lust

Basquiat's rebellion

He was a man who'd found his peace

Hard won from a stifling childhood

An artworld anomaly

And how does that reconcile with the artist temperament

I would ask and ask and ask the gods

I asked my father once after he had retired from his career

why he no longer painted

Not for work but for personal reward

Something he had always done

I feared an answer that would obliterate

any art-centered spirit

Some horrible *"I just wanna play golf from now on"* sentiment

When he responded that in being a family man he no longer had

the crucial solitude required to turn inward for the task

I found myself elated and restored

In spite of whatever smidgen of melancholy might've actually

lingered in him from the claim

As if what I needed from my father more

than art

was merely the assurance

of artist

Holy Order

the figures in black

instruct / each of us

takes a handle

of the nylon sack / oblong

like a canoe / his

closing heraldry /

a belt loop for each

pair of hands / nearly cutting

our palms

our psalms

souls bleed / instead of flesh

sons daughters wives

we march the lion out / heavy in death

as do troops their leader

from the battlefield

his battlefield his bedroom

no one speaks

no one looks

no one breathes

he is the folding of the flag

he is the bugle sounding taps

the nylon canoe sails away with our lion inside

he is / the forever that we need

Motion Sickness

How does it feel to be a laughingstock?
the entire world asks me about my nation in
an interview that my mind's Theatre of the
Absurd invents and replays every day.

My father is diagnosed with congestive heart
failure, an additional diagnosis to his already
flourishing Alzheimer's, merely days before
a new commander-in-chief is sworn into office.
The meme "not my president" swirls constantly
inside that theatre, alongside conversations
about hospice and end-of-life measures.
My world is folding in on itself like a failed
soufflé. OUR world feels on a similar course,
though I find myself mute to the public
forum conversations, as I see my friends on
social media bitterly divided about a man
whose name I have a hard time saying.

My father's name, by comparison, is hailed
by the many in my little world. I brag on his
achievements on Facebook even more now
that he is about to leave us, and pray for his
art, which I constantly post, to drown out all
the warring rhetoric of *libtards* and *sheeple*

that flood my computer screen with images
of swirled color instead, strokes made from
brushes and palette knives, heart expressed
in the glorious realm of the abstract. And even
the friends of mine who stunningly live on the
opposite side of my most deeply held beliefs
join me in lauding the art of my father. And
the symbolism is about as subtle as the
man in the oval. And I don't care. I embrace
the heavy-thudded clubfootedness of it.

And the rarely fixed always erratic state of
the White House dances rather artfully with
the never again fixed increasingly erratic
state of My Father's House. An uprising.

And the swirls of vertigo madness and
gashes to my inner ear are so fraught with
the wild and the dangerous and the allusions
to a Van Gogh sky or a Munch scream,
drenching Awful in alluring Mood and
Memory, as to be almost beautiful.

The Starting Bell

How could the man
who rear-ended my
car in a cowardly hit-&-run
the day after the most
heartbreaking Christmas
I've ever had
possibly know that he was
sounding the starting
bell of a spell so
concussed with
collision that to this
day my neck has never
quite snapped back
into place?

In this way he operates
as symbol as mountain
as face-to-face
encounter with
a grizzly.
The kind of thing where
If you live to tell the story
it wreaks of epiphany

and transformation.

Keeps literary this miscreant

too unworthy to make literary.

Too small to anoint

with words

yet here we are.

He is a poem...

Tomorrow

Tomorrow isn't promised, they say.

We could die tonight and

never see another sunrise.

But it will rise,

the sun.

We might not, but the sun always will.

When we are lowered into the earth

with ceremony and pomp

and wreckage and tears,

newspapers will still be

hurled onto lawns.

Milk will still go bad in fridges.

People will fall in love.

People will fall out.

They will remember us.

They will forget us.

They will be the ones,

the only ones,

who can imbue memory

of who we were

in this life

onto history.

To stamp us into time.

And what they say

will be shaped

by what we've done.

Flesh will fall away from our bones

down there in the deep deep earth

and tomorrow is still promised.

For all whom we've left behind

to mourn us

to rage

to forgive

to let go

it will come rushing

like a pushed up earth by the sprig of new life.

Bones

The bones that provide the structure around which his sinews grow,
that carry his muscles & nerves, that make his hands & fingers, which
hold the artist's brush, do miraculous things on a woven canvas, paint
saturating the weaves, color folding in on color, indigo naming pain,
dusted sage reporting on triumph, blood red breaking a heart, as blood
red will do, are cracking, are growing brittle, are finding their final place.

The bones that attach to each other by ligaments, that are fattened &
strengthened by marrow, that cleave to flesh, that make a merry bed
where love is large & family is made & offspring assure legacy &
history, are holding together edematous legs, but tenuously, are
collapsing beneath the awesome shadow of time.

The bones that carry pain, that lash out at innocents, that make
a cradle for tears, that brace for punishment & atonement &
forgiveness, are settling in on each other, succumbing to gravity &
mortality, are learning to rest, making a crib for organs to nestle &
say goodnight, having done their job here, in just under a century.

The magnificent precious bones have done their job here.
& magnificently.

Angela Carole Brown is the recipient of the North Street Book Prize in literary fiction for her novel *Trading Fours*, and the SoulWord Magazine Poetry Prize for her poem "Cotton Candy." She is also the author of the novel *The Assassination of Gabriel Champion*, the memoir *The Kidney Journals: Memoirs of a Desperate Lifesaver*, the 100-word story collection *Aleatory on the Radio*, and the poetry chapbook *Viscera*. She writes the blog Bindi Girl Chronicles. She has also been on the L.A. music scene for over three decades as a singer, songwriter, and recording artist, has produced several albums of music in the genres of jazz and folk, and is the lead singer in Elvis Schoenberg's Orchestre Surreal. She is featured in the documentary film *The Goddess Project*. *Bones* marks her first full-length poetry collection.

www.angelacarolebrown.com
www.bit.ly/BooksByAngelaCaroleBrown
Facebook @angelacarolebrown
Instagram @bindigirlchronicles
Twitter @angelacarolebro

www.ingramcontent.com/pod-product-compliance
Lightning Source LLC
Chambersburg PA
CBHW060120050426
42448CB00010B/1957